THE IMPLICATIONS OF MISSION

Study by Amy Costantini Cook
Commentary by Cecil Sherman

Free downloadable Teaching Guide for this study available at
NextSunday.com/teachingguides

NextSunday Resources
6316 Peake Road
Macon, Georgia 31210-3960
1-800-747-3016
©2022 by NextSunday Resources
All rights reserved.

TABLE OF CONTENTS

The Implications of Mission

HOW TO USE THIS STUDY

NextSunday Resources Adult Bible Studies are designed to help adults study Scripture seriously within the context of the larger Christian tradition and, through that process, find their faith renewed, challenged, and strengthened. We study the Scriptures because we believe they affect our current lives in important ways. Each study contains the following three components:

Study Guide

Each study guide lesson is arranged in four movements:

Reflecting recalls a contemporary story, anecdote, example, or illustration to help us anticipate the session's relevance in our lives.

Remembering provides a frame of reference for the Scriptures.

Studying is centered on giving the biblical material in-depth attention while often surrounding it with helpful insights from theology, ethics, church history, and other areas.

Understanding helps us find relevant connections between our lives and the biblical message.

What About Me? provides brief statements that help unite life issues with the meaning of the biblical text.

Commentary

Each study guide lesson is accompanied by an additional, in-depth commentary on the biblical material. Written by a different author than the study guide, each commentary gives the opportunity for learners to approach the Scripture text from a separate but complementary viewpoint.

Teaching Guide

In addition to the provided study guide and commentary, *NextSunday Resources* also provides a *free* downloadable teaching guide, available at NextSunday.com. Each teaching guide gives the teacher tools for focusing on the content of each study guide lesson through additional commentary and Bible background information. Through teacher helps and teaching options, each teaching guide also provides substance for variety and choice in the preparation of each lesson.

NextSunday
Resources

STUDY INTRODUCTION

When we hear the word "mission," we immediately think about crossing the globe to spread the Word of God, and we feel helpless. We find ourselves trapped in lives and schedules and commitments that are difficult to change, so we leave the "mission work" for those who do it vocationally.

But what does it actually mean to be "missional"? The term "mission" comes from the Latin *mitto*, which means "to send." God is a sending God, the One who sends all Christians to live in praise and glory of God. Ephesians 1:8b-12 describes our calling this way: "With all wisdom and insight he has made known to us the mystery of his will, according to his good pleasure that he set forth in Christ, as a plan for the fullness of time, to gather up all things in him, things in heaven and things on earth. In Christ we have also obtained an inheritance, having been destined according to the purpose of him who accomplishes all things according to his counsel and will, so that we, who were the first to set our hope on Christ, might live for the praise of this glory."

Many have tried to define the sacred task of being a missionary. Carl Braaten, a Lutheran Theologian, for example, wrote, "Mission is understood as the function of the Kingdom of God in the world's history." W. O. Carver wrote that "Missions mean the extensive realization of God's redemptive purpose in Christ by means of human messengers." These claims certainly encompass what it is to be a "missional" Christian, but my favorite definition is one by friend and former professor of Christian Mission, Dr. Isam E. Ballenger: "Mission is participation in the Trinity. Thus, it cannot be 'defined,' for definitions will be insufficient; mission breaks the bounds of any limitation. Mission is thus not a program of the church but is fundamental to the nature of the church. It is the life of the church. It begins with doxology and flows from blessings received."

According to Dr. Ballenger, we are all capable of missions at all points in our lives, wherever we may live. When we are in Christ, missions is not something we go somewhere else to do; it becomes a part of who we are. Whether we are doctors, lawyers, teachers, storekeepers, fast food workers, stay-at-home caregivers, retired, or unemployed, being "mission-minded" is foundational to the Christian life. In this way, we are all missionaries.

WHAT'S IN AN ACT?

Mark 9:38-48

Central Question

Who is called to missions?

Scripture

Mark 9:38-48 John said to him, "Teacher, we saw someone casting out demons in your name, and we tried to stop him, because he was not following us." 39 But Jesus said, "Do not stop him; for no one who does a deed of power in my name will be able soon afterward to speak evil of me. 40 Whoever is not against us is for us. 41 For truly I tell you, whoever gives you a cup of water to drink because you bear the name of Christ will by no means lose the reward. 42 If any of you put a stumbling block before one of these little ones who believe in me, it would be better for you if a great millstone were hung around your neck and you were thrown into the sea. 43 If your hand causes you to stumble, cut it off; it is better for you to enter life maimed than to have two hands and to go to hell, to the unquenchable fire. 45 And if your foot causes you to stumble, cut it off; it is better for you to enter life lame than to have two feet and to be thrown into hell. 47 And if your eye causes you to stumble, tear it out; it is better for you to enter the kingdom of God with one eye than to have two eyes and to be thrown into hell, 48 where their worm never dies, and the fire is never quenched."

Reflecting

It had been a long day. As the only chaplain on staff at a hospice in-patient facility, I was tired. I tried to bring spiritual peace and hope to the dying and their families, but I unintentionally felt I was the only one there who had adopted that role. I was wrong.

During my conversation with the family of a patient, another employee joined us. She, too, ministered to this family, bringing them words of comfort and spiritual hope. In one of my weaker moments, I spoke up in disagreement with the theological viewpoint my fellow employee expressed. It was an embarrassing situation for both of us and disgraceful (in the literal sense of the word) of me. I'm not sure what came over me; maybe it was a territorial issue, but I've been careful not to do it again.

That situation, while difficult, was helpful to me because it reminded me that Christ calls many people to work in his name. We are to work *with* one another to bring hope to people in need. It is easy to let our feelings and ambitions become obstacles when we try to minister to others. I was not the only one at the hospice that day capable of being a minister, and I am grateful to work with so many people who hear and respond to God's call. The hospice staff was there before me. Long after I leave, they will still be there providing care and effectively ministering to others in need.

Remembering

During the late sixties of the first century AD, Christians in Rome endured volatile times. They had heard much about Jesus from firsthand witnesses to his teachings, but many eyewitnesses had died. Emperor Nero persecuted Christians in his attempt to cleanse Rome from this upstart religion. This is traditionally considered the setting of the Gospel of Mark.

The writer of Mark, likely the first person to write a Gospel, ensed an urgency to record the events of Jesus' life. Eyewitnesses were aging, so those with firsthand experience would soon be unavailable to validate the good news of Christ's salvation message. Christians' relied on oral tradition to pass on and share stories and information. While the oral tradition worked well for centuries, once Christians' lives were in danger, there was a risk that no one would survive to continue the Christian tradition. This gospel—the mission of Jesus—had become a part of who they were, and it was something for which they were willing to give their lives. Thus, Christians needed to record these words for future generations.

> Oral Tradition: "The passing along of the biblical material by word of mouth, prior to the writing down of these materials—narratives, poetic utterances, wisdom sayings, lists and the like" (Harrelson, 634).

Studying

Mark 9:38-41 The events of this lesson's text occur just after the twelve disciples finish arguing about who is the greatest among them (vv. 33-37). Even the disciples were concerned about their social status! Jesus explained that the one who would be first among them must be last and servant of all. He further explained that as disciples we should all welcome others, even children, into our lives.

However, the actions of the disciples in the next few verses contradict Jesus' teachings. Jesus was advancing God's mission. Later, in the words of the Great Commission (Mt 28:19), he instructed the disciples to go to the four corners of the earth to teach the nations of his glory, giving authority to humankind to heal and prophesy in Jesus' name. When John proudly informed Jesus of the disciples' recent encounter with those who were not following them, Jesus probably shook his head as he saw yet another teachable moment. It is interesting that this event occurs right after the disciples' argument over greatness. John's opinions are clear as he proudly discounts others' authority to act in Christ's name. Jesus, however, was more interested in what John pointed out: when Jesus' name was invoked, demons were cast out (v. 38). Obviously, others were aware of and believed in the power of Jesus' name, and Jesus' mission advanced.

Jesus has faith in each of us, as children of God, to work for good in Jesus' name. We must use the power of Jesus' name constructively and effectively as we work to share God's love in the world. The power to do good in Christ's name is not to be monopolized by a single class or type of believers. It is important for us to bear witness to the tolerant spirit of Christ: "Do not stop him...for truly I tell you, whoever gives you a cup of water to drink because you bear the name of Christ will by no means lose the reward" (vv. 39-41). With the responsibility of sharing the gospel comes Christ's expectation that we respect each other's efforts and encourage the other's success. After all, we are taught that one of the greatest commandments, second only to loving God with our whole selves, is to love our neighbor as ourselves (Mk 12:30-31). This implies not only love but also action, and we are called as Christians to act in love toward our fellow neighbor.

The disciples' words and actions are evidence of the long history of church politics. Jesus' disciples thought they were the authority on the truth and that only they were capable of doing anything in Jesus' name (v. 38). After all, they walked shoulder-to-shoulder with the Messiah. However, Jesus rebuked his disciples by introducing a new proverb: "Whoever is not against us is for us" (v. 40b).

As Christians, we are charged with acting in Christ's name. If we are to spread the word of God effectively, we must trust others with this task as well. It is ironic that the exorcism upset the disciples. Not much earlier in their ministry (vv. 14-29), the disciples themselves tried to perform an exorcism in Jesus' name and could not do it. Is it any wonder, then, that they wanted to prevent someone else from succeeding at this task? Even Jesus' disciples, like the rest of us, were competitive in nature. But thanks be to God, who continues to entrust us with the task.

Mark 9:42-48 In the same way that Jesus sought to include all who believed in him and in doing good in his name, he rebuked the disciples for trying to prevent anyone, especially the "little ones" (v. 42), from teaching and learning about him. It is significant that a child sat on Jesus' lap (v. 36), for children were not regarded nearly as highly as they are today. In the same way that it was taboo in Jesus' time for a Jew to speak with a Samaritan woman (Jn 4:7-9), it was also unheard of to acknowledge a child. Regardless of the many translations for "little ones," the significance of this phrase is clear: No one is insignificant in Jesus' eyes.

No one is exempt from the love of God, and we are called to treat others accordingly.

In verses 43-47, Jesus points out chief instruments most commonly used for sin: the hand, the foot, and the eye. Humankind lifts the hand to do violence, as did Cain against his brother Abel (Gen 4:8). We use our feet to run from God's calling to do what is right, as did Jonah (Jon 1:1-3). Our eyes cause us to sin, as did King David when lusting after a married woman, Bathsheba. This sin caused a series of others, among them the murder of Bathsheba's husband, Uriah (2 Sam 11:2-27). The last instrument, the eye, may be the most dangerous because of its threefold potential for sin: to hurt others and ourselves, to trespass against others and God, and to covet. Jesus said, "The eye is the lamp of the body. So, if your eye is healthy, your whole body will be full of light; but if your eye is unhealthy, your whole body will be full of darkness" (Mt 6:22-23a).

Jesus tells us that if these body parts are stumbling blocks, it is better to sever them from our bodies, our holy temples (1 Cor 6:19), than to be thrown into hell. Of course, Jesus was not telling us literally to cut off our body parts, but he used this common metaphor to prove the gravity of his point. Craftsmen and agricultural laborers, who comprised the majority of the population during Jesus' time, commonly injured these specific body parts. The original audience was also familiar with stories of Greek mythology. Jesus' stories and figures of speech were common metaphors and offered illustrative images for the disciples to under-

The word used for "hell" (in vv. 44-47) in the original Greek was *Gehenna*. This name was given to a particular valley located south of Jerusalem. Offal and filth were usually cast into this wasteland, and the people set fire to the valley in order to burn what they threw away. In turn, these deposits that were useless to humankind were set apart from Jerusalem forever (Exell, 374).

The Greek *Mikron Touton*, translated "little ones" in verse 42 and commonly assumed to be in reference to children, is a term Jesus used. However, Jesus often used this phrase in referring to Christians in general (Mt 18:10, 14) (Perkins, 640) and when referring to the marginalized (10:17-31) (Senior and Stuhlmueller, 213).

stand. The idea of losing a body part to avoid causing oneself or another to stumble had become proverbial by Jesus' time; and Jesus, a master educator, used the most suitable terms possible to ensure coherent communication.

Understanding

In this passage, Jesus challenges us to look inward at our true motivations in working for God. Are we truly interested in bringing others to Christ, or are discipleship and piety merely status symbols? Are we so eager to take ownership of all the good works of God that we cannot allow a fellow pilgrim to join us in Jesus' name?

Therefore lift your drooping hands and strengthen your weak knees, and make straight paths for your feet, so that what is lame may not be put out of joint, but rather be healed. (Heb 12:12-13)

O taste and see that the LORD is good; happy are those who take refuge in him. (Ps 34:8)

Yet, O LORD, you are our Father; we are the clay, and you are our potter; we are all the work of your hand. (Isa 64:8)

Jesus knows that all of us are made in God's image, and all of us are capable of doing God's work. As Jesus pointed out to the disciples, "Whoever is not against us is for us" (v. 40).

Scripture challenges us to use our feet (Heb 12:12-13), our eyes (Ps 34:8), and our hands (Isa 64:8) as God-given tools for spreading the word of God. Jesus included all who desired to be in his circle. As Christians, we must learn that people are at different places in the Christian journey. Everyone, even "little ones," needs to experience the love of Jesus Christ. We can all be instruments in making this happen. Are we willing to give others a try?

What About Me?

• *We are all on the outside.* The outside is a place where we are outcasts, a place in our lives where we feel like no one around us hears or cares. We all experience this terrifying and lonely feeling.

• *We are all on the inside.* Because of our experiences, positive and painful, and because of our Christlike image, we are all capable of helping others feel accepted and loved. In turn, we learn what it means to be a true follower of Christ.

• *One cannot be a Christian and not be concerned about missions.* Missions encompassed the whole of Jesus' life on earth. To neglect that part of him in our everyday lives would be to reject much of what it truly means to be a Christian.

• *Each of our actions has the power to bless.* When we remember our power and responsibility to bless others with our actions, we honor Jesus' example.

Resources

David J. Bosch, *Transforming Mission, Paradigm Shifts in Theology of Mission* (Maryknoll NY: Orbis Books, 1991).

Joseph S. Exell, *The Biblical Illustrator* (Grand Rapids MI: Baker Book House, 1988).

Walter Harrelson, "Oral Tradition," *Mercer Dictionary of the Bible*, ed. Watson E. Mills et al. (Macon GA: Mercer University Press, 1990).

Pheme Perkins, *The Gospel of Mark*, The New Interpreter's Bible (Nashville: Abingdon Press, 1995).

Donald Senior and Carroll Stuhlmueller, *The Biblical Foundations for Mission* (Maryknoll NY: Orbis Books, 1983).

WHAT'S IN AN ACT?

Mark 9:38-48

Introduction

This session's text has at least three parts. Here's what I see:
(1) The disciples were concerned that people not of their circle were "casting out demons" in the name of Jesus (Mk 9:38a). John (and other disciples) "tried to stop him, because he was not following us" (9:38b). How wide is the Christian circle? What should our attitude be toward "irregular" people who speak in the name of Jesus?
(2) Jesus gives an answer that stretches our tolerance. Who is doing Christ's work? Christian deeds have to be taken into account when we are deciding who is and who is not "of Christ."
(3) Finally, there are two "warnings":
• Be warned about harming the faith of others, "these little ones." If I cause them to stumble, I put my soul at risk.
• Be warned about harming my own faith. To lose faith is worse than to lose a hand, a foot, an eye. To hold on to faith is more important than to be whole in body.

The title of the session highlights v. 41: "Whoever gives you a cup of water to drink because you bear the name of Christ will by no means lose the reward." I will spend my time commenting on John's question and Jesus' answer.

Over one hundred and fifty years ago, J. R. Graves, a persuasive editor of a Baptist paper in Tennessee, questioned whether Baptists ought to allow Presbyterians, Methodists, and Disciples in Baptist pulpits. He questioned whether these denominations were churches at all. He granted that a Methodist was a member of a "Christian society"; he did not believe a Methodist was a member of a "church" in the New Testament sense of the word.

In those days, Baptists, Methodists, Disciples, and Presbyterians competed for membership. The "church" that could convince people that it was the "true" church was the denomination most likely to gain support and loyalty. All groups claimed the Bible and argued from it. All groups had their champions in debate. From our perspective, all groups made fools of themselves. This is the painful truth: All who took part in those contentious times thought they were serving Christ. The bad feeling from that Christian competition lingers in some quarters. This is one illustration of the fences we've built around our churches. This subject speaks to our need, and I'm glad for a chance to comment on it.

I. What Should We Do with Irregular Jesus People? 9:38-40.

John voiced a concern of the disciples. An unnamed "someone" outside the immediate circle of Jesus was "casting out demons in your name [Jesus], and we tried to stop him, because he was not following us" (9:38). Apparently the man was having success, but the disciples were disturbed that the man used "the name of Jesus" since he was not of the approved company of disciples. Before coming down too hard on the disciples, let me play "devil's advocate."

John may have had good reasons for asking his question. Scripture speaks of "false prophets." The early church wrestled with those who taught heresy. I suspect John was concerned that "the name of Jesus" not be misused.

Interestingly, the "someone" was able to do what the disciples had been unable to do. Earlier in Mark 9 a man brought his son to Jesus for healing. He introduced himself: "Teacher, I brought you my son; he has a spirit that makes him unable to speak...and I asked your disciples to cast it out, but they could not do so" (9:17-18). "Someone" was close enough to the spirit and power of Jesus to heal; sometimes the disciples were not.

The answer Jesus gave to John's question needs to be heard: "Jesus said, 'Do not stop him; for no one who does a deed of power in my name will be able soon afterward to speak evil of me. Whoever is not against us is for us' " (9:39-40). We need to hear this word. Many strong denominations go take the "we can go it alone" approach. They don't need to cooperate with other Christians, and they even hold themselves aloof from most ecumenical efforts. What Jesus said raises a question about our position.

By now you may be wondering, "Is this the meaning of this text or is this just Cecil Sherman's opinion?" It is my opinion, but I am not alone in the way I've interpreted the text. Here's what other commentators say:

• Frederick C. Grant said our text is "a warning against exclusiveness and overemphasis upon apostolic authority" (*The Interpreter's Bible*, vol. 7 [New York: Abingdon Press, 1951], 789).

• Halford E. Luccock said, "The point of this plea (the plea for inclusion) is timeless. It says to us, 'Take a wide view of your faith instead of a narrow one' " (ibid.).

• William Barclay wrote, "It is necessary always to remember that truth is always bigger than any man's grasp of it. No man can possibly grasp all truth" (*The Gospel of Mark* [Philadelphia: Westminster Press, 1956], 233).

• Henry Turlington said, "Jesus abruptly rejected John's spirit of intolerance. 'Do not forbid him' means, You are wrong: stop hindering him. Why? Because, although he is not now one of us, his mind is at least favorably disposed and open" (*The Broadman Bible Commentary*, vol. 8 [Nashville: Broadman Press, 1969], 344).

It is not to our credit to withdraw from other parts of the Christian community or be judgmental of them. There are places in the Bible that stress correctness of doctrine; these texts need to be factored in to specific situations. But the sense of Jesus is openness. He was open to sinners. He was open to women. He was open to Gentiles. And he was open to people who used his name even when they did not have his permission to do so. Jesus told his disciples, "Do not stop him; for no one who does a deed of power in my name will be able soon afterward to speak evil of me" (9:39). In these days denominations have divided over countless issues. If Jesus would not shut down the work of an exorcist who was borrowing his name, would he call home a missionary over a doctrinal statement? Jesus gave people room to think. What should we do with irregular Jesus people? Nothing.

II. Simple Acts of Kindness Identify Jesus People, 9:40-41.

Two rules surface here. They standardize the attitude we are to have toward people who are in some way identified with Christ but not "of us."

(1) "Whoever is not against us is for us" (9:40). Most of us have grown up in a society where Christians are all around. This text would be read with different eyes were we Christians in Iran or Indonesia, where there aren't many Christians. In America it seems Catholics and Baptists are different; in Indonesia, both are called "Christian," and both may be discriminated against for it.

At the end of my basic seminary training (1954), I went outside Baptist life to study at Princeton Theological Seminary. The school is sponsored by Presbyterians, but there were all kinds of Christian groups in the student body. I was one of two Baptists in a seminary of about four hundred. Dot and I took three meals a day with Christians from all over the earth; that intense time with people who were not from the South, who were not Baptists, informs this session. I learned firsthand that there are many good people in God's service.

(2) "Whoever gives you a cup of water to drink because you bear the name of Christ will by no means lose the reward" (9:41). To understand how this verse fits into the session, let's try to crawl into John's situation. He had been sent out on a preaching mission. The disciples were out in the open, preaching in streets and fields. Sometimes people welcomed them, but just as often they were ignored or taunted. Jesus told them to live off the land: "Take no gold, or silver, or copper in your belts, no bag for your journey, or two tunics, or sandals, or a staff; for laborers deserve their food. Whatever town or village you enter, find out who in it is worthy, and stay there until you leave" (Mt 10:9-12). Those were the instructions; it was a life built on faith.

Now back to the text. Who were your friends? Jesus' way of identifying friends was practical: "Whoever gives you a cup of water to drink because you bear the name of Christ will by no means lose the reward" (9:41). The sense of the text is this: The people who help you are with you. A cup of cool water will identify a friend—and a friend of Christ.

Much has been made of God the bookkeeper. When I was a boy I was told God kept record of my idle words, my deliberate sins, and my accidental missteps. This gave me pause. God was keeping score, and "at the last day," God would open the books and bring my sorry record to light. That idea of God still haunts me occasionally.

This text tells us God is a bookkeeper, but the nature of God is altogether different from what I was told as a child. Halford Luccock said, "Jesus provides us here with the true picture of that divine bookkeeper. In his recordings even the slightest service of kindness and love is a tremendous item to be entered. Even a cup of cold water is big business and goes down on the credit side" (*The Interpreter's Bible*, vol. 7, 790).

No mention is made of theology as a test. No word is in the text about "spiritual food." All that is cited is real water by people who were at the margins of the Christian company. Whoever they were, they just helped Christ's people as they did Christ's work. And they did it in the most down-to-earth, practical way. These people who gave the "cup of water" were outsiders; they are nameless in the New Testament. Pheme Perkins said of them, "Such outsiders will also receive a reward. Unlike the scribes and Pharisees, Jesus seeks to draw the boundaries between those who are 'with Jesus' to include as many people as possible" (*The New Interpreter's Bible*, vol. 8 [Nashville: Abingdon Press, 1995], 639).

This has been a session on tolerance and inclusiveness. I've had to think about these ideas a good bit the last few years. In 1 John this subject is addressed: "Beloved, do not believe every spirit, but test the spirits to see whether they are from God; for many false prophets have gone out into the world. By this you know the Spirit of God: every spirit that confesses that Jesus Christ has come in the flesh is from God, and every spirit that does not confess Jesus is not from God" (1 Jn 4:1-4a).

There are basic theology and basic practice. Confessing Jesus is basic theology; that's the only thing that is grounds for exclusion. A "cup of water" is basic practice; it is meeting people at the point of their need. That's what Jesus did, and that's where we ought to be. What's in an act? It's not complicated at all; it's a cup of water for people who bear the name of Jesus. That's it.

Notes

Notes

A GOD WHO ACTS IN TIME

Exodus 19:7-15; John 1:14-18

Central Question

How can we incorporate God's example of preparation and constant care into our living?

Scripture

Exodus 19:7-15 So Moses came, summoned the elders of the people, and set before them all these words that the LORD had commanded him. 8 The people all answered as one: "Everything that the LORD has spoken we will do." Moses reported the words of the people to the LORD. 9 Then the LORD said to Moses, "I am going to come to you in a dense cloud, in order that the people may hear when I speak with you and so trust you ever after." When Moses had told the words of the people to the LORD, 10 the LORD said to Moses: "Go to the people and consecrate them today and tomorrow. Have them wash their clothes 11 and prepare for the third day, because on the third day the LORD will come down upon Mount Sinai in the sight of all the people. 12 You shall set limits for the people all around, saying, 'Be careful not to go up the mountain or to touch the edge of it. Any who touch the mountain shall be put to death. 13 No hand shall touch them, but they shall be stoned or shot with arrows; whether animal or human being, they shall not live.' When the trumpet sounds a long blast, they may go up on the mountain." 14 So Moses went down from the mountain to the people. He consecrated the people, and they washed their clothes. 15 And he said to the people, "Prepare for the third day; do not go near a woman."

John 1:14-18 And the Word became flesh and lived among us, and we have seen his glory, the glory as of a father's only son, full of grace and truth. 15 (John testified to him and cried out, "This was he of whom I said, 'He who comes after me ranks ahead of me because he was before me.' ") 16 From his fullness we have all received, grace upon grace. 17 The law indeed was given through Moses; grace and truth came through Jesus Christ. 18 No one has ever seen God. It is God the only Son, who is close to the Father's heart, who has made him known.

Reflecting

I went to college at a large public university. I was excited to be on my own for the first time, ready to tackle the world. I remember sitting in my economics class during freshman year and feeling lost in the class of 150 students. The professor did not know my name on the first day, nor did he know it on the last.

Four years later, I first entered the halls of seminary. While my freshman class in college numbered about 3,000, my first-year class in seminary was slightly less than 50! Most of the faculty and staff knew my name and even stopped in the hallways to speak with me. Monthly listening sessions provided the opportunity for all students, faculty, and staff to congregate and share personal and academic joys and concerns.

In my course on Christian missions, we learned that "God is a God who acts in time: One who sent, sends, and will send again; One who came, comes, and will come again." At seminary, I experienced a continuing sense of God's love and deliberate care exhibited through others.

Remembering

Exodus 19:7-15 This passage, which directly precedes the presentation of the Ten Commandments, is often overlooked. God gave Moses specific directions to prepare for the giving of the Law. Moses was to follow these directions in reverence of the approaching time of worship.

God makes a habit of sending leaders, just as God sent Moses to lead the Israelites. After Moses freed the Israelites from the bondage of Pharaoh in Egypt, the people wandered in the wilderness for many weeks. Moses brought structure to the thousands of people and, at the urging of his father-in-law, appointed heads over various groups to settle small disputes (Ex 18:17-27). By the beginning of chapter 19, the Israelites have reached Sinai, where they are about to encounter God's presence for the first time. The Israelites had acquired a sense of living in community, and God was ready to give them the Ten Commandments and officially establish these people as God's chosen ones. Before the holy event could take place three days later, however, the people had to prepare.

John 1:14-18 The Gospel of John is believed to be the last of the four Gospel accounts. Written near the end of the first century, this Gospel differs from the other three. Most scholars believe the author wrote this Gospel to establish Jesus' identity as the Son of God. The writer of John focuses more on Jesus' divine identity

God intentionally took time and care to plan each day of creation and each creative act that occurred within it. Days four, five, and six each contain creations that were perfectly made to inhabit the parts of the earth created in days one, two, and three, respectively (Balentine).

than his earthly one. In the first fourteen verses, for example, the writer establishes Jesus' connection with God.

The whole book of Exodus is an account of a God who will not let God's people go (indeed, this theme carries throughout the Bible). From bondage in Egypt to despair in the wilderness and finally to hope at the sight of the promised land, the Israelites saw God work in their lives. Across the pages of the New Testament, we continue to see God sending others (even God's self incarnate) to serve as a guiding force in carrying out God's desire to redeem humankind.

Studying

God is a God of patience. Across the ages, God has used the natural course of events—within the boundaries of earthly time—

to accomplish God's plan. We see evidence of divine timing from the beginning of Scripture, when God created the world (Gen 1:1–2:3). Though God is all-powerful, capable of creating this world in one moment, there was a method—a rhythm—to God's creation.

God was even deliberate in staying within the natural course of human events after deciding to destroy creation with the flood and begin the world again. God called Noah and gave him seven days to build an ark. A little less than a year later, Noah and his family began their lives on earth again. Our God is intentional, acting purposefully and taking time in getting things done.

How do you prepare yourself to worship God?

Exodus 19:7-15 In this Scripture, God stresses the importance of what is about to take place (the presentation of the Ten Commandments, Ex 20). God's deliberate planning for this pivotal event is obvious. Verses 7-15 serve as the hinge between what the Israelites already were and what they would become. God appointed a time for the revelation of God's self and the commandments to humankind. God's instruction led the Israelites to treat the presentation of the Ten Commandments with great respect.

God instructed Moses to consecrate the people twice (vv. 10, 14) in order to prepare them to be in God's presence three days later. This practice of ritual washing was an essential element of preparation for worship (30:17-24), and God's command to do it set the giving of the Law apart from events in their past (Brueggemann, 836). This would not be a regular day for the Israelites. God would be in their presence, bestowing upon them guidelines for life. This would be an act of worship. God

The LORD spoke to Moses: "You shall make a bronze basin with a bronze stand for washing. You shall put it between the tent of meeting and the altar, and you shall put water in it; with the water Aaron and his sons shall wash their hands and their feet. When they go into the tent of meeting, or when they come near the altar to minister, to make an offering by fire to the LORD, they shall wash with water, so that they may not die: it shall be a perpetual ordinance for them, for him and for his descendants throughout their generations." (Ex 30:17-21)

set aside a holy moment to remind the Israelites of God's constant love and guidance.

John 1:14-18 In the beginning of the Gospel of John, God is described as one who acts in the interest of humanity across the ages, always finding yet another way to be an active part of our lives. What better way to be involved in the lives of humankind than to be born of a woman (Lk 1:21-35) and experience life on earth firsthand?

Our God came to this earth to "dwell" among us. This Greek verb shares a root word with the Hebrew noun for "tabernacle," which was used in the book of Exodus when God spoke to Moses and when God's glory was seen (Ex 33:9; 40:34). This word, alluding to Israel's Sinai experience, was the first of many images included in the prologue ("glory," v. 14c; "law," v. 17; Moses, v. 17). In the same way that God was always with the Israelites, so God continues to be with us. The Gospel of John makes no mistake: "The law indeed was given through Moses; grace and truth came through Jesus Christ" (v. 17). It is impossible to separate the law from grace and the Sinai experience from the birth of Jesus (O'Day, 522). God actively participated in all these experiences, and continues to participate with those whom God calls. The writer of John magnificently connects the Sinai experience to the birth of Jesus, showing that the same God who journeyed with the Israelites through all their hardships is the same God who continues in our lives today, birthing new beginnings to guide us.

Understanding

When you receive a gift from a friend, would you rather it be one casually thrown into the shopping cart or one that your friend chose with care and effort? "It's the thought that counts."

Sometimes we say this because we are not thrilled with the results of a gift or situation. However, if we know that love and deliberate preparation are behind it, it can sometimes mean more to us than a wonderful gift that resulted from an afterthought.

"Tabernacle" is referred to a number of times in the Hebrew Scriptures (Ex 28:43; Num 16:26-27). For a time, the tabernacle was the centralized place of worship for the Israelites. While they were on their sojourn at Sinai, "God commanded Moses to construct a portable sanctuary wherein [God] might dwell. The Tabernacle was to become the primary center of Israel's communion with her God throughout the ensuing three hundred years until a more permanent center could be built" (Maltsberger, 871).

Throughout these passages of Scripture are countless examples of God's deliberate thought, love, and care poured into each decision. God was well aware of the timeless significance of the presentation of the Ten Commandments, even though the Israelites had no idea what they were being prepared to receive. Moses showed us the care that God put into each decision and event, and the Israelites responded with reverence: "Everything that the LORD has spoken we will do" (Ex 19:8). The Israelites witnessed a holy moment—the product of God's careful preparation for this worshipful event—that proved to change the ways in which we relate with one another and our God forever.

Where have you seen God alive throughout your daily routine? It is amazing that we are held so tightly by a loving God (Gen 8:20-22). God masterfully uses the time line of humanity to become more and more visible in our lives. Throughout the pages of Scripture, we see the footprints and fingerprints of God, left as evidence of God's constant care for humanity. We are called to try to be like God with the time and care we give to our everyday lives. When we do this, we act as God's people, and this brings glory to God.

What About Me?

• *How intentional are you about reaching out to others?* As Christians, we go to worship for renewal, but *outside* our church building walls, through our daily routines, we truly find our mission field.

• *Being a constant in people's lives is important.* Exposing people to the love of Christ is our mission, but our mission is enriched when we walk beside others in their Christian journey.

• *Trust God.* This is easier said than done, but we can be confident that God has gone before us, and this same God will continue long after we leave the earth. No one else can offer God's perspective. Time after time, God proves to be reliable and loving.

Resources

Dr. Samuel Balentine, "Introduction to Old Testament," course notes, 1999.

Dr. Isam E. Ballenger, "Introduction to Christian Missions," course notes, 2000.

Walter Brueggemann, *The Book of Exodus*, The New Interpreter's Bible (Nashville: Abingdon Press, 1994).

David C. Maltsberger, "Tabernacle," *Mercer Dictionary of the Bible*, ed. Watson E. Mills et al. (Macon GA: Mercer University Press, 1990).

Gail R. O'Day, *The Gospel of John*, The New Interpreter's Bible (Nashville: Abingdon Press, 1995).

A God Who
Acts in Time

Exodus 19:7-15; John 1:14-18

Introduction

This session is about the nature of God. Here is a compressed version of a heavy subject:

(1) There are two positions people can take on God. One group says they don't believe in God at all or they say they don't know whether there is a God or not. The other group believes there is a God.

(2) We are the people who believe there is a God. Our Scriptures begin, "In the beginning when God created" (Gen 1:1a). This is our first faith assumption; all others flow from it.

(3) What did God do then? Again, there is a difference of opinion:

• One group believes God created heaven and earth and then stepped back. God views but does not enter into what we do.

Deism is not of the ancient world; some of the founders of our nation were Deists (most notably Thomas Jefferson). Deists argue that God set laws in place that govern the universe, but God is not concerned with the day-to-day affairs of life. Deists say God "does not interfere." The title of our session is "A God Who Acts in Time." The Deist would say God does not act in time.

• Christians believe God acts in time. We believe the single decisive act of God was when Jesus came. The New Testament part of our text makes this point. Philosophers call our religious point of view "personalism." God knows us and sometimes acts to save us from ourselves; often, God acts to motivate us to high service.

(4) A fourth issue has nothing to do with philosophy or history. Some people agree that God acts in time—IN THE BIBLE! Functionally, these people are Deists. They come to church and

pray, but they don't expect God to do anything. They would argue that the time when God did those things has passed; we are on our own in life. This session has a message for such people. God not only acted in time, but God continues to act in time. God not only spoke to them, but God continues to speak to us. God used Hebrews and apostles, and God wants to use us today.

"A God Who Acts in Time" requires a large stage. The outline I offer will use more Scripture than usual. This session is about the Christian view of the nature of God. I will paint with a broad brush.

I. A God Who Cares.

Early in Scripture the nature of humankind is defined. Genesis 3 tells the story of Eve, the serpent, and the forbidden fruit. The sense of the story is that our parents sinned and sin separated them from God. God was not content with this separation. God acted to remove the sin (Noah and the flood). Still, sin grew like weeds in God's garden. There had to be another way to get at the problem.

In Abraham, Bible history turns a page. God called (Gen 12:1-3) and made a covenant with Abraham (15:1-21). Abraham and his children would be instruments of God for good: "In you all the families of the earth shall be blessed" (Gen 12:3b). God wanted to use Abraham's family to deliver a message. Don't get lost in the detail; the session is about God. God initiated the idea and came to Abraham. The reason God called Abraham was because God cared. When Abraham's descendents had multiplied, gone into Egypt, and become slaves, they turned to God: "Out of the slavery their cry for help rose up to God. God heard their groaning, and God remembered his covenant with Abraham, Isaac, and Jacob. God looked upon the Israelites, and God took notice of them" (Ex 2:23b-25).

We don't pray "Our Father, who art in heaven" for nothing. In the prayer there is a vision of God. God is our heavenly parent; therefore, God does what good parents do: God loves us; bothers with us. When God moved Moses to go into Egypt and free the enslaved Hebrews, God was acting in time. That's how the Exodus part of our text connects to this part of the session.

II. A God Who Makes Covenants.

Is God knowable? Can we get a fix on the character of God and organize our thoughts about God? Partly. We can't "put God in a box," but Scripture tells us God is willing to make agreements called covenants: "Many interpreters view the covenant concept as the cord that binds the various parts of the Old Testament together" (Page H. Kelley, *Exodus: Called for Redemptive Mission* [Nashville: Convention Press, 1977], 92). Covenant means "bond or fetter." There were two kinds of covenants:
• A covenant between equals is illustrated in the friendship that grew into a covenant between David and Jonathan.
• There were also covenants between the greater and the lesser: an agreement between a king and his subjects illustrates this idea.

God's covenants with Israel were of the second type. A strong God made covenant with a needy people. God made covenant with Noah and with Abraham. Our Exodus text tells about an agreement God made with the nation. As Page Kelley beautifully says, "Israel was to be the pilot project in God's plan to redeem all nations. In choosing her, God was establishing a beachhead in human history from which he would never be dislodged until his worldwide purpose had been achieved" (Kelley, *Exodus: Called for Redemptive Mission*, 95-96). It was a grand idea. Israel would be "a priestly kingdom and a holy nation" (Ex 19:6). God had not only saved them from slavery, but God had great plans for their future.

The Exodus text is one of the turning points in the Old Testament. The people of Israel were assembled at the foot of Sinai. God gave special instructions about how they were to "consecrate" themselves for the occasion (see 19:10-15). On the third day God broke in: "There was thunder and lightning, as well as a thick cloud on the mountain, and a blast of a trumpet so loud that all the people who were in the camp trembled. Moses brought the people out of the camp to meet God" (19:16-17a). It was grand and awesome. Nobody who was there ever again wondered if "God acted in time." No argument changed their minds; it was experience.

Much has changed in our understanding of God since Sinai, but one thing remains constant: Experienced religion is the only kind that changes lives. I can tell you about God, but until you experience God you probably remain unconvinced.

III. God Notices Covenant Failure.

At this point I depart our texts and venture deep into the Old Testament. Abraham's children became Hebrews; Hebrews became Jews. Days came and went; years hurried by. Tribes became a nation. A tabernacle became a temple. David made Israel great. Division and poor choices made Israel disappear; Judah just managed to survive. Babylon came and destroyed Jerusalem and the temple; the leaders were taken captive. Where was God? How could this happen to a chosen people who were in covenant with a great God?

The prophets give us the answer. Hebrews were brought low because they forgot the covenant their parents made with God. They chased after other gods, forgot their agreements, and God punished them. The story of Hosea is personal and painful. As Hosea's unfaithful wife went off after other lovers, so Jews went off after other gods. They had made sacred promises and broken them. Jesus did not come because God was happy with the arrangement he had with the Jews. He came because God was not happy. The covenant made in Exodus 19 was wasted.

This part of the session is not easy reading. God's prophets gave a clear message that the people had to change. They did not change, and God judged them. Preachers speak of "the unconditional love of God." If they mean there is no sin God will not forgive, they are right. If they mean you and I can sin repeatedly—without remorse or intent to change—*and* God will do nothing, they are choosing to omit a sad picture of broken covenants. There is judgment. Captivity was judgment for Judah and the Jews. God acted in time. God judged a people.

IV. A God Who Tries Again.

John's Gospel has no nativity story. We don't read about Bethlehem, Mary and Joseph, shepherds, or wise men. Our text is from "the prologue." John tells us about the coming of a Savior who had been with God from creation, who was an agent in creation. He describes Christ as "the Word." God had spoken words to humankind before; this time "the Word became flesh and lived among us" (Jn 1:14a). God was trying a new way to make contact with confused, lost children. The plot of the Bible is this: After a failed experiment with covenant (Ex 19), God tried again. The coming of Jesus was a new way to approach an old problem. How can God reconnect with humankind? The covenant was a good idea that could have worked. One side in the covenant agreement did not keep its promise. However, God did not give up on us. God tried again in Jesus. Several strong ideas come out of John's prologue.

(1) God is raising the bar. In the past God spoke to wayward people through prophets. In Christ, God sent God's Son: "We have seen his glory, the glory as of a father's only son" (1:14b). Jesus is a higher, later revelation than previous acts of God had been. Jesus told a story about a man who planted a vineyard; it appears in Matthew 21:33; Mark 12:1; and Luke 20:9. That parable makes the same point John's prologue is making.

(2) John the Baptizer testified of Jesus and prepared the way for him. Some thought John the Baptist was the messiah; this was a mistake. John's revival was grand, but it was preparation for what God was doing in Jesus: John testified about Jesus, "This was he of whom I said, 'He who comes after me ranks ahead of me because he was before me'" (1:15b).

(3) Grace trumps law. The law served a useful purpose. Paul said it best: "The law was our disciplinarian until Christ came" (Gal 3:24a). When Christ came, whole sections of the law were put aside. As law took pagans and elevated them, so grace took rule-keepers and raised them to a higher plane: "The law indeed was given through Moses; grace and truth came through Jesus Christ" (1:16). We know God better through the grace of Christ than we know God through the rules of Moses.

(4) God is hard to know. Remember the scene with God speaking to Moses from atop Sinai? God was shrouded in smoke and spoke in thunder and lightning. That kind of God is daunting, awesome, other: "No one has ever seen God" (1:18a). However, in Jesus Christ, God put on another face. The Old Testament God who sometimes terrified became more approachable: "It is God

the Only Son, who is close to the Father's heart, who has made him known" (1:18b).

Did God change, or did our understanding of God change? I don't think God changed, but our understandings of God did. God was always caring of other nations even when God had "chosen" the Jews. God always intended salvation for Gentiles. God was always scheming a way to penetrate our thick-headedness and to win us to God's self. That's what this text is saying.

Notes

Notes

HISTORY IS
NOT MEANINGLESS
Matthew 1:1-17

Central Question

How do we use our history as a guide for being instruments of
God's divine mission?

Scripture

Matthew 1:1-17   An account of the genealogy of Jesus the
Messiah, the son of David, the son of Abraham. 2 Abraham was
the father of Isaac, and Isaac the father of Jacob, and Jacob the
father of Judah and his brothers, 3 and Judah the father of Perez
and Zerah by Tamar, and Perez the father of Hezron, and Hezron
the father of Aram, 4 and Aram the father of Aminadab, and
Aminadab the father of Nahshon, and Nahshon the father of
Salmon, 5 and Salmon the father of Boaz by Rahab, and Boaz
the father of Obed by Ruth, and Obed the father of Jesse, 6 and
Jesse the father of King David. And David was the father
of Solomon by the wife of Uriah, 7 and Solomon the father of
Rehoboam, and Rehoboam the father of Abijah, and Abijah the
father of Asaph, 8 and Asaph the father of Jehoshaphat, and
Jehoshaphat the father of Joram, and Joram the father of Uzziah,
9 and Uzziah the father of Jotham, and Jotham the father of Ahaz,
and Ahaz the father of Hezekiah, 10 and Hezekiah the father of
Manasseh, and Manasseh the father of Amos, and Amos the
father of Josiah, 11 and Josiah the father of Jechoniah and his
brothers, at the time of the deportation to Babylon. 12 And after
the deportation to Babylon: Jechoniah was the father of Salathiel,
and Salathiel the father of Zerubbabel, 13 and Zerubbabel the

father of Abiud, and Abiud the father of Eliakim, and Eliakim the father of Azor, 14 and Azor the father of Zadok, and Zadok the father of Achim, and Achim the father of Eliud, 15 and Eliud the father of Eleazar, and Eleazar the father of Matthan, and Matthan the father of Jacob, 16 and Jacob the father of Joseph the husband of Mary, of whom Jesus was born, who is called the Messiah. 17 So all the generations from Abraham to David are fourteen generations; and from David to the deportation to Babylon, fourteen generations; and from the deportation to Babylon to the Messiah, fourteen generations.

Reflecting

A friend of mine from college is one of two children. His mother lives with her husband of twenty-six years in a small town in the Midwest, and he is the product of a happy home. Of course, my friend and his mother have their differences; sometimes he gets frustrated when she does not listen to him as intently as she could or when she interrupts him.

Despite his frustrations, my friend loves and respects his mother. She raised two children, made a wonderful career for herself, and, with her husband, provided well for her children. However, there is so much more to her than most people know.

She grew up in a household where her mother believed being a female was less than adequate. Her only brother was given many opportunities that she did not receive, and at times she felt like an outcast in her own home. To make matters worse, her mother was an alcoholic, so my friend's mother left home after high school. College was not an option for her. She did not receive much of the positive attention, encouragement, and love that we all need from our mothers, especially during childhood.

Despite her circumstances—and maybe because of them—she has become a wonderful, caring, and attentive mother. It is amazing how she was able to look back at her childhood, tell herself that she would be different, and actually follow through with that goal! She still wrestles with remnants from her past, but through the years my friend has witnessed in his mother an admirable and respectful love and inner strength.

Our family history, or genealogy, plays an important role in our lives. My friend has learned to try to understand his mother's past before becoming frustrated with her present actions. He has also learned how strongly our families, even from many generations ago, affect and enrich our lives and personalities. Our personal histories shape us into the people we are today, and they reveal more about us than we can imagine.

Remembering

The author of Matthew was Jewish and wrote for a church with a Jewish tradition and membership, like most early Christians. Matthew mentions the temple frequently (21:12, 23; 24:1) as well as the importance of keeping the Sabbath (12:1-4; 24:20). The author does not explain the importance and reasons behind these traditions, so readers today must assume that the original audience was already familiar with Jewish customs and laws. Therefore, scholars assume that the audience of the Gospel must have been Jewish Christian. Matthew's genealogy offers his Gospel more validity while serving as a smooth bridge that connects the Hebrew people's journey and tradition with the story of salvation.

Studying

For the people of ancient times, history and tradition were important. Read the book of Numbers for a taste of the preservation of family history. It is no wonder, then, that the author of Matthew included a long genealogy within this text, placing it before something in history as pivotal as the birth of the Messiah. Verses 1-17 offer a host of clues about Jesus as well as the people to whom Matthew was writing.

An explanation of the first verse could consume pages of study: "A record of genealogy" (v. 1), literally a "book of genesis" (*biblos genessos*), is a phrase full of possible meanings. In using the term "genesis," the author of Matthew seems intentionally to allude to the book of Genesis. In the same way that the book of Genesis marks the beginning of history, Matthew intended this

Gospel to mark the coming of Christ, an event that would represent the new creation, the renewal of all things (2 Cor 5:17).

Also in this verse, the author refers to Jesus as both the "Son of Abraham" and the "Son of David." Though it can be read in different ways, it seems these are not literal genealogical designations but simply titles given to Jesus. Especially throughout the Gospel of Matthew, we see Jesus referred to by both titles (9:27; 12:23). Any reference to the Son of David is a messianic title (acknowledging Jesus as the Messiah). On the other hand, "Son of Abraham" is not a messianic title but is used to authenticate Jesus' position as heir to the promises of God made to Abraham (Boring, 125-26). Abraham did not know God when God called him and promised that he would be the father of many nations (Gen 12:1-3; 17:5). God sent Jesus for all of humanity. Therefore, when the author of Matthew included Abraham in his genealogy, his intention was to assure his audience that the promises of God are for all of creation, not exclusively the Jewish people (3:9; 8:11; 22:32).

> Now the LORD said to Abram, "Go from your country and your kindred and your father's house to the land that I will show you. I will make of you a great nation, and I will bless you, and make your name great, so that you will be a blessing. I will bless those who bless you, and the one who curses you I will curse; and in you all the families of the earth shall be blessed." (Gen 12:1-3)

The rest of the genealogy reveals much about Jesus as well as Jesus' culture. This genealogy was written more to place Jesus' birth in the context of the continuing acts of God than to record an account of history.

The text separates into three periods: (1) the kingship of David (vv. 2-6), (2) the deportation of the Israelites to Babylon (known as the Babylonian Exile, vv. 6-11), and (3) the birth of the Messiah (vv. 12-16). First are

> The exile, in which part of Judah was taken into the land of Babylon, occurred around 598 BC (2 Kgs 24:1-17). Though their living conditions were not extremely harsh, the Jewish people were still prisoners in a foreign land, and their faith was challenged. From this torment, however, a faith developed that has proven to be strong enough not only to survive but to prosper under any conflicting circumstance or law (Dunston, 276).

the stories of King David and the rise of Israel as a great Jewish nation. Then comes the exile, where the nation lay naked in its shame and disaster. Finally, we learn of a man who liberated people from slavery and disaster, turning tragedy into triumph, death into life (Barclay, 13-14). In these verses, we see a picture of a God who builds us up, allows us to make mistakes, and then walks by our side out of love and mercy. Our God has not changed. History continues to show us how God can use each of us for good.

The grace of God is clear in this sacred genealogy. Many of those listed have questionable reputations: Jacob was known for his deception; David had a man killed (Uriah); Tamar, pretending to be a prostitute, conceived her father-in-law's child (Gen 38); Rahab was a prostitute (Josh 2; 6:22-25). Regardless of their reputations, these individuals later proved exceedingly loyal to God and to the Law (Barr, 260). From them, we learn that God can use all people, even those who fall from grace.

Also important is the mere mention of women. It was not common to include women in genealogies, so the author of Matthew took a chance to illustrate something profound: contrary to popular belief, women were important and could serve God equally well. Even more significant is the suggestion that there is something different about this upcoming birth; the genealogy of the Messiah, of all people, included women—and they were Gentiles!

The entire list foreshadows Jesus' earthly ministry of inclusion and equality. Just as Jesus was a radical in his time, so was the genealogy that led to his birth.

Understanding

At the climax of this genealogical list of Jews and Gentiles, men and women, sinners and saints, we read of the birth of the most perfect person on earth. Though the author of Matthew wrote for a Jewish audience, the book includes and celebrates all people as recipients of the promises and mercy of God. History tells us that even 2,000 years ago, in a patriarchal society, women had a place in the story of the birth, life, death, and resurrection of Jesus.

Most of all, history teaches us, even challenges us, to use the palette of our history to shade in the colors of our future. As followers of God, it is important to see where our theological roots are planted so that we may better understand ourselves and the God who made us. Only then can we understand how to be people on mission for God.

What About Me?

• *In Matthew, the genealogy connects Jesus with the long history of God's activity*. It reveals Jesus as the promised one of God's mission.

• *The mercy of God extends to all people—not just ourselves*. All of humanity can be used as effective instruments in the furthering of God's kingdom. It is our role to have faith in ourselves, each other, and in God so that God use each of our gifts fully.

• *How has your past affected your present relationships?* Though we don't always realize it, our past plays an important role in how we act toward others. Our behaviors are rooted in the different threads of the fabric of our history.

Resources

William Barclay, *The Gospel of Matthew*, vol. 1 (Philadelphia: Westminster Press, 1975).

David L. Barr, *An Introduction, New Testament Story* (San Francisco: Wadsworth Publishing Company, 1995).

M. Eugene Boring, *The Gospel of Matthew*, The New Interpreter's Bible (Nashville: Abingdon Press, 1995).

Robert C. Dunston, "Exile," *Mercer Dictionary of the Bible*, ed. Watson E. Mills et al. (Macon GA: Mercer University Press, 1990).

HISTORY IS
NOT MEANINGLESS

Matthew 1:1-17

Introduction

When I saw our text, I thought my editor had made a mistake. Could I really be expected to write a commentary on a genealogy? With some frequency the Bible has a long list of unpronounceable names; those are the parts we skip. And now a lesson from a genealogy! I was amazed but not amused. How in the world can I find meaning in these verses? Even more daunting, how can I put enough salsa on this text to make it tasty? Then I began to read about genealogies in the Bible, and the subject became a little clearer.

Early Hebrews did not attach importance to genealogies: "Early Hebrew family records (Ex 35:30) reach only to the 'third and fourth generations' (Ex 20:5). As late as the Persian period, only once in the Jewish Aramaic papyri does identification of a witness reach the fourth generation" (*The Interpreter's Dictionary of the Bible*, E–J [New York: Abingdon Press, 1962], 363). But that changed.

After captivity, Ezra and Nehemiah put great store on Jewish purity. Jews had been scattered after "the fall of Jerusalem" (587 BC). Priests were required to prove they were Jews and that they were not soiled by intermarriage with Gentiles. With the requirement for "proof" of purity came other reasons for genealogies:
• individual identity for legal purposes—like inheritance
• nobility had to establish their "rights"
• demonstration of relationship to important events or people

What puts us off and makes for hard reading actually attracted Jews of the first century. If I were setting out to write a "life of Jesus," I would not begin as Matthew did. But Barclay put it this way: "It might seem a daunting proceeding to present the reader right at the very beginning of his book with a long list of names to wade through. But to a Jew this was the most natural, and the most interesting, and indeed the most essential way to begin the story of any man's life" (*The Gospel of Matthew*, vol. 1 [Philadelphia: Westminster Press, 1958], 1).

I majored in history in college; I teach history and am biased about it. I think history is undervalued in our educational programs. Some of my intelligent students are unlearned about church history; they hardly know the rudiments of American history. My family doesn't know or care about genealogy. I can name my grandparents only to the fourth generation. Evidently they held Henry Ford's opinion of history. In July 1919, Ford brought a libel suit against the *Chicago Tribune*. He was asked about history and made a remark that has become famous. Ford said, "History is bunk." Jews didn't think so, and their genealogies bear witness to a sense of who they came from, who they were, and where they were going. We need to know what the genealogy of Jesus meant to the Jews who read it, *and* we need to see if it has meaning for us.

I. The Genealogy of Jesus Connects.

Jesus was a Jew. To Matthew's audience, this idea had powerful appeal. Jews knew their history. To be descended from Abraham meant you were a Jew. To be descended from Abraham through David meant your pedigree was tip-top. There are forty-one generations cited, but "the rabbis would have regarded Abraham and David as the high points in the genealogy" (Sherman E. Johnson, *The Interpreter's Bible*, vol. 7 [New York: Abingdon Press, 1951], 251).

The sense of the genealogy was to "connect" Jesus to important people in Jewish history *and* to "connect" Jesus to Jewish expectations. The Messiah was expected to come from the line of David, and Matthew tells us Jesus was.

The idea that Jesus was of David means little to me; so when I see it in the New Testament, I take no notice of it. However, David's relationship to Jesus is a theme in the New Testament.

• At Pentecost, Peter said, "Fellow Israelites, I say to you confidently, of our ancestor David that he both died and was buried…. He knew that God had sworn…that he would put one of his descendants on his throne" (Acts 2:29-30). Peter was connecting Jesus to David and to the destiny God had in mind for the Jews.

• Paul's letter to the Romans begins, "Paul, a servant of Jesus Christ, called to be an apostle, set apart for the gospel of God, which he promised beforehand through his prophets in the holy scriptures, the gospel concerning his Son, who was descended from David according to the flesh" (Rom 1:1-3). Note the connection to David.

• The New Testament closes with a vision of John: "It is I, Jesus, who sent my angel to you with this testimony for the churches. I am the root and the descendant of David, the bright morning star" (Rev 22:16).

• Matthew does not leave the "son of David" connection to genealogy. He repeats it. Crowds were amazed at Christ's ability to heal and exclaimed, "Can this be the Son of David?" (12:23b). A Canaanite woman shouted at Jesus, "Have mercy on me, Lord, Son of David; my daughter is tormented" (15:22). Two blind men at Jericho shouted, "Lord, have mercy on us, Son of David!" (20:29-30). Near the end, as Jesus entered Jerusalem for the last time, the crowds "went ahead of him…shouting, 'Hosanna to the Son of David!' " (21:9).

Jesus was connected to people who had the highest standing in Jewish life; he was qualified to be the Messiah. That's the point Matthew set out to make.

II. The Genealogy of Jesus Interprets.

Frank Stagg sees in the genealogy an interpretation of the history of the Jews: "The overriding concern of the genealogy is to trace the fortunes of God's people from the great expectations of Abraham to the seeming fulfillment in David (vv. 2-6), then the decline from David to the Babylonian exile, where all seemed to be lost (vv. 7-11), and finally from the hopelessness of the Babylonian exile to the true goal in Jesus Christ (vv. 12-16)"

(*The Broadman Bible Commentary*, vol. 8 [Nashville: Broadman Press, 1969], 81).

William Barclay sees the same thing. In a section he titles "The Three Stages," Barclay says the genealogy is arranged in three stages:

(1) Verses 2-6a tell of the generations from Jesse, father of David. This part "takes the story up to the rise of Israel's greatest king" (*The Gospel of Matthew*, vol. 1, 3).

(2) Verses 6b-11 tell a story of decline: "And Josiah the father of Jechoniah and his brothers, at the time of the deportation to Babylon" (1:11).

(3) Verses 12-16 end like this: "And Jacob the father of Joseph the husband of Mary, of whom Jesus was born, who is called Messiah" (1:16). Abraham was given a promise of glory for Israel. It appeared King David fulfilled the promise; that appearance was dashed in Babylon. Jesus came to restore Jewish destiny.

There is a hopefulness that runs deep in the Bible. God is making sense of the maze and the confusion that is life. The story of humankind is going toward endtime, judgment, and eternity. All sorts of interpreters of history are around us. Cynics hold that history moves toward oblivion. Christians see the hand of God in it. Sometimes we can make no sense of it. In those dark times a Christian holds tight to faith. "We know that all things work together for good for those who love God, who are called according to his purpose" (Rom 8:28) is still in the Bible. Matthew was telling his first readers (and us) that God is in history and will make sense of it.

III. The Genealogy of Jesus Includes.

The first point went to some length to point out the "connections" of Jesus. To get the attention of a Jewish audience, Matthew could not have cited better credentials. However, the genealogy includes more than heroes. Note the types in this most interesting list of names.

(1) There were four women. This was unusual: "Remarkable is the inclusion of four women (Tamar, Rahab, Ruth, and the wife of Uriah). Customarily, Jewish genealogies give only the names of

men" (Stagg, *The Broadman Bible Commentary*, vol. 8, 81). It is remarkable that women were in the genealogy; it is more remarkable when you consider who they were. Rahab was a harlot of Jericho. Ruth was a Gentile. Tamar was no saint; pretending she was a harlot, she tricked her father-in-law into getting her pregnant with twin sons. Bathsheba (Uriah's wife) committed adultery with David. So although Jesus came of Abraham and King David, there were parts of his background much like yours and mine.

(2) Kings other than David are mentioned—Hezekiah, Manasseh, and Josiah. Hezekiah and Josiah were "the good kings." The sacred writers describe Manasseh as wicked; he led Israel into idolatry. There is no whitewashing in the list.

(3) Then there are ordinary people. Some of the names listed appear no other place in the Bible. Abraham Lincoln's line fits: "God must like ordinary people; he made so many of them." Most of the people in the genealogy were "just folks." (It should be noted that this genealogy is not complete. All commentators note that there are not enough names to stretch across the years. Stagg says, "His purpose is to relate Jesus to David and Abraham, not to give a literal and complete genealogical catalog" [ibid.].) Spliced in among the great were plain people. Jesus was born to a plain young woman, Mary. Joseph was a carpenter. Just folks.

(4) The genealogy of Jesus implies the Holy Spirit: "And Jacob the father of Joseph the husband of Mary, of whom Jesus was born, who is called the Messiah" (1:16). George Buttrick said, "No human birth, however royal, can account for Jesus; he came by the direct and creative act of God. There is a mystery in Christ which human factors alone cannot explain" (*The Interpreter's Bible*, vol. 7, 252). A child of Joseph and Mary, even if descended from Abraham and King David, could not do what Jesus did. The source for Jesus has to go back to God.

IV. The Genealogy of Jesus Looks Forward.

Our text reads, "An account of the genealogy of Jesus the Messiah, the son of David, the son of Abraham" (1:1). The word for "genealogy" in the New Revised Standard Version can be

translated several different ways. Here is how other translations have rendered this verse:
• The King James Version—"The book of the generation of Jesus Christ"
• The Revised Standard Version—"The book of the genealogy of Jesus Christ"
• J. B. Phillips—"This is the record of the ancestry of Jesus Christ"
• The New English Bible—"A table of the descent of Jesus Christ"

All these versions struggle with Matthew's word "genesis" (the same word that names the first book in the Old Testament). Literally, the word means "beginnings." In Jesus, God is picking up the pieces of a sad history, pushing them to the side, and starting over again. Jesus is a fresh start for God and therefore for us.

The idea of starting over again appears often in the Bible. Sometimes it seems God is not so much starting over as moving forward: "Long ago God spoke to our ancestors in many and various ways by the prophets, but in these last days he has spoken to us by a Son, whom he appointed heir of all things" (Heb 1:1). God was raising the bar in revelation. In Jesus we could see more of what God was like and what God wanted of us.

Life is like this genealogy. It moves forward and upward. Even death is not final. God is not finished with us. God has more in mind. Always, God is working with a future tense. If God is looking forward, we ought to be looking forward too.

I found more in "the genealogy" than I expected. Most important is the subtle, hopeful interpretation of history in it. History is not meaningless. God is in it. That is a faith statement: "In Christ God was reconciling the world to himself" (2 Cor 5:19). That's was Matthew tells us in the genealogy.

Notes

Notes

THE HUMAN
RESPONSE
2 Corinthians 5:16-21

Central Question

What is our responsibility to missions?

Scripture

2 Corinthians 5:16-21 From now on, therefore, we regard no one from a human point of view; even though we once knew Christ from a human point of view, we know him no longer in that way. 17 So if anyone is in Christ, there is a new creation: everything old has passed away; see, everything has become new! 18 All this is from God, who reconciled us to himself through Christ, and has given us the ministry of reconciliation; 19 that is, in Christ God was reconciling the world to himself, not counting their trespasses against them, and entrusting the message of reconciliation to us. 20 So we are ambassadors for Christ, since God is making his appeal through us; we entreat you on behalf of Christ, be reconciled to God. 21 For our sake he made him to be sin who knew no sin, so that in him we might become the righteousness of God.

Reflecting

Dr. Charles B. Bugg wrote in the dedication of *Getting on Top: When Life Gets Us Down*, "The most profound sermons are those that are practiced, not preached." I experienced this type of "sermon" during Vacation Bible School. Children came from different parts of the community for this special week, and many of the children did not know each other.

One particular morning, about thirty preschool children sat on the floor, listening to their leaders. One young girl struggled with being in a new place and missing her family. The leaders were taking care of her, trying to make her feel better. Hunter, a young boy who had grown up in the church, noticed this girl. When he approached her, one of the leaders asked him to sit down. He was determined, however, and when he reached the little girl, he gave her a hug. As he walked back to his seat, he said to the leader, "She looked like she needed a hug."

Children can often teach us something profound about being Christlike in our actions. St. Francis of Assisi is remembered for his many contributions to Christian spirituality, but arguably his most famous and poignant words are these: "Preach the gospel always; if necessary, use words."

Remembering

When we meet Paul in 2 Corinthians, he is defending himself and his teachings to the people of Corinth. Paul was devoted to the

Corinthian church. Since his revelation on the road to Damascus (Acts 9:1-9), Paul's mission was to spread the word of Jesus and be an example of Christ for others (Gal 2:19-20).

The Corinthian church was comprised of Jews and Gentiles all trying to adhere to the Christian way. The people were like toddlers who constantly question new experiences and interpret them in their own ways. They tried to live as a Christian community while still living their lives the way they preferred. Because they were still learning the ways of Christ, the community did not fully trust in or adhere to Paul's teachings. When Paul's opponents entered the community, teaching a false religion and opposing much of what Paul had taught them, the Corinthians fell deeper into turmoil. It was a time of confusion and anxiety for them. Paul corresponded with them often in response to their questions, comments, and accusations of the authenticity of his teachings. Second Corinthians is traditionally believed to be a compilation of several pieces of correspondence Paul wrote.

Studying

In the verse preceding this lesson's passage (v. 15), Paul reminds the Corinthian community that Christ died for all people. In response, we are all called to live as Christ would. We have become a "new creation" (v. 17).

With this transformation comes great responsibility. What does it mean that Christ died for all of us? Paul first tells us we must view our neighbor as Christ would. We may no longer look back to former ways of living because our eyes have been opened to new life in Christ. If we look back, we reject Christ's gift. Once we are

"For the love of Christ urges us on, because we are convinced that one has died for all; therefore all have died. And he died for all, so that those who live might live no longer for themselves, but for him who died and was raised for them." (2 Cor 5:14-15)

Christians, the old life is gone. We are charged to see others the way Christ sees us. The standards of judgment set in place from the beginning were radically changed, and we are now called to see this change as a commission from God to be changed people with a new way of seeing and understanding.

Paul tells us we are a new creation in Christ. To be "in Christ" means to live in intimate relationship with him. There is a difference between being *in* Christ and being *with* Christ. Paul tells us we are often guilty of relating to Christ the way we relate to our colleagues, class-mates, and fellow church members. But how about our best friend, a close family member, or a spouse? We experience a deep level of intimacy when we share feelings and seek goals together, and we are changed people because of them. This is what it means to be *in* Christ. The transformation takes place within our souls. To open ourselves to the fullness of Christ's spirit and he to ours is to live *in* Christ (Exell, 292).

In verse 16, Paul tells us that we no longer view others "from a human point of view." This is better translated as "according to the flesh" (*kata sarka*). Therefore, Paul is saying that when we look at others, we should not see simply what is seen with the human eye (4:18; 5:7), but we are urged to see people for who they are on the inside. Our appearances do not show what is in our hearts (5:12) (Sampley, 92-93).

Further, Paul's use of the expression "new creation" (*kaine ktisis*) explains how becoming a Christian is a renewal of our entire being. This phrase clearly illustrates recapturing, not replacing, the old and transform-ing it into something beautiful. Paul knew the anger and frustra-tion within the Corinthian community and toward him would slowly dissipate once they realized the power of Jesus' transforming love.

Leviticus 21:11 reads, "He shall not go where there is a dead body; he shall not defile himself even for his father or mother." To be *in* Christ, we are a new creation. God is a God of life, and we are called to be these new creations. If we were to retreat to our old ways of life, it would be an abomination to the life that we are called to live in Christ.

What are we commissioned to do? Verses 19-20 teach us that if we are one in Christ, then the "message of reconciliation" is entrusted to us. Paul calls us ambassadors for Christ. It is no wonder that Paul brought this message of reconciliation to the Corinthian church at this time. Strife and hostility were alive and well in their own lives. Paul challenged the people to be ambas-sadors for Christ, taking with them the message of reconciliation, because he knew that in order for this turmoil to end, they must

take the first step. It was their turn to "put on the breastplate of faith and love, and for a helmet the hope of salvation" (1 Thess 5:8b).

Interestingly enough, verse 20 is the only place in Paul's letters where he urges others to be reconciled to God, which is traditionally a task God initiates toward us. It is plausible that Paul wanted the people to take the initiative in this situation in an attempt to persuade the Corinthians to be reconciled toward him. Since Paul was aware of the negative feelings of those who had turned against him, it is possible that Paul hoped to win them back. He may have appealed to them by reminding them of their significance in Christ's name and that it was he who brought this gospel of reconciliation to them in the first place (Sampley, 95).

Understanding

Paul was a man convicted by his beliefs, feeling the heavy burden not only to spread the good news of Jesus Christ but to expect to see a difference in the people's lives! We have all heard these sayings: "Easier said than done." "Better you than me." "You can talk the talk, but can you walk the walk?" Paul's admonition to accept the gift of salvation and live it outwardly is difficult at times, but Paul was clear in his message that once Christ enters our lives, our lives should reflect the change.

With the change, however, comes a partner in Christ. It is difficult always to see others the way Christ would see them; it is difficult always to act in a pleasing way. But when we become Christians, Christ accepts us, as couples pledge in their wedding vows, for better or for worse. We are allowed to mess up; it is important that we try to be better people. With Christ living within us, we have a guide to help us through every situation. We are not left alone in the divine task of changing the world and ourselves; we receive the gift of each other and the constant presence of Christ.

What better person to preach this message of sin and reconciliation than Paul, who once dedicated his life to the persecution of Christians? After he allowed Christ into his life, he did not simply believe and continue to live the way he always had. He underwent a massive transformation so that he no longer saw people in earthly ways (Gal 1:13-17). Of course, we know that even Paul could not act like Christ all the time, but we are called to work on this task each day of our lives.

There is a huge task before us. Scripture teaches us to believe in God, and we are even instructed on how to live. As if that weren't enough, we are now given a reason why this new way of life is so important: "The old has passed away; see, everything has become new!" (2 Cor 5:17). The new creations we become are people in Christ, going forth not only to "talk the talk, but walk the walk." We are ambassadors for Christ. We are Christians, and there is no other response to this call than to see the world from Christ's point of view and live our lives accordingly.

What About Me?

• *Love God and live like it.* The Bible teaches us in various ways that it is not enough simply to love God; we need to show this love through our actions.

• *How often do we expect others to prove to us their value?* Christ died for us all, regardless of whether or not we choose to accept this. All of us are of value to Christ, and we are all called to see others as Jesus does.

• *Followers of Christ make the world a better place.* Imagine a world where people regard Christianity as a way of life. The power to make this happen lives in each one of us.

Bibliography

Dr. Charles B. Bugg, *Getting on Top: When Life Gets Us Down* (Nashville: Broadman Press, 1990).

Joseph S. Exell, "2 Corinthians," *The Biblical Illustrator* (Grand Rapids MI: Baker Book House, 1988).

J. Paul Sampley, *2 Corinthians*, The New Interpreter's Bible (Nashville: Abingdon Press, 2000).

THE HUMAN RESPONSE

2 Corinthians 5:16-21

Introduction

Does history have meaning? The Bible says yes. Is history moving toward a defined end? The Bible says it is. Do individuals have a part to play in history? That's the subject for this session.

Paul wrote a second letter to the Corinthian church to outline God's design of redemption, but interwoven in that grand theme is Paul's request that they honor him as an apostle. It is difficult to believe that some people did not think Paul qualified to be a church leader, but such people existed. They thought Paul overly zealous, given to religious ecstasy. Paul defended himself: "For if we are beside ourselves, it is for God; if we are in our right mind, it is for you. For the love of Christ urges us on" (2 Cor 5:13-14a).

William Barclay recalled a story about Rudyard Kipling and General Booth, founder of the Salvation Army. Kipling and Booth were aboard the same ship. A group of tambourine-beating Salvationists had seen Booth off on his journey. The whole scene revolted Kipling's soul. Later, Kipling got to know the general and told him how much he disapproved of this kind of behavior. "Young man," said Booth, "if I thought that I could win one more soul for Christ by standing on my hands and beating a tambourine with my feet I would learn to do it" (*The Letters to the Corinthians* [Philadelphia: Westminster Press, 1956], 232). The real enthusiast does not care if others think he is a fool.

This kind of attitude in Paul brought forth the sentence, "The love of Christ urges us on" (5:14a). Why was Paul driven to the ends of the ancient world telling people about Jesus? Love. Paul's love for humanity was a reflection of the love that drove Jesus from heaven to earth. Paul borrowed from the love of God in

Christ, took on some of the nature of Christ himself, and spent himself telling people about Jesus. Did he sometimes look like a fool? Probably. Our text tells us Paul had come to a new way of looking at things. When he became "a man in Christ," Saul became Paul; what was once unthinkable became appropriate. Everything changed.

God acted in history when Jesus came into the world. Jesus grew and John baptized him. He healed, gathered disciples, and came into conflict with the established religious order. They framed and killed him. Then God raised him up; that's what Easter is about. The risen Christ appeared to Saul of Tarsus on the road to Damascus. The persecutor of the church became a missionary for the church. He was changed. Paul was not a careless man; he pondered what had happened to him. Our text is the reflection of a mature Christian. He described what happened to him and what ought to happen to all who come to Christ. If you think about what Jesus has done for us, what should our response be?

I. A New View of Christ, 5:16, 18-19a.

"From now on, therefore, we regard no one from a human point of view; even though we once knew Christ from a human point of view, we know him no longer in that way" (5:17). "Regard" means to make an evaluation based on human estimates. Floyd Filson helped me here. He said, "From a human point of view is to judge them by external situation and standards, without a true understanding of their worth and place in God's sight; in particular, as applied to Christ, it means to think of his lowly life and shameful crucifixion as proof that he was disowned by God and so should be rejected my men" (*The Interpreter's Bible*, vol. 10 [New York: Abingdon Press, 1953], 336-37).

Let's suppose Saul of Tarsus was in Jerusalem on the Passover when Jesus was crucified (the supposition is unlikely). G. R. Beasley-Murray put it this way: "The same man, the same cross, the same crowd and the same dark sky would have been in view; but Saul would have seen a blaspheming pretender justly suffering the judgment of God" (*The Broadman Bible Commentary*, vol. 11 [Nashville: Broadman Press, 1971], 41). That's the way

Saul of Tarsus saw Christ before the Damascus Road experience and that's a *human* point of view on Jesus.

When Saul was on his way to Damascus to stamp out Christians, Jesus Christ appeared, spoke to him, and changed him at the deepest level. Conversion changed Paul's estimate of Jesus. Knowing about Jesus is one thing. Knowing Jesus is different. John Wesley was sailing to Georgia to do church work. On board were Moravians. A Moravian asked Wesley, "Do you know Jesus?" Wesley said, "I know that he is the Savior of the world." "Yes," said the Moravian, "But do you know him?" (James Reid, *The Interpreter's Bible*, vol. 10, 338). Later at Aldersgate Chapel on a cold, wet night, Wesley felt his heart "strangely warmed." From then on he had a different point of view on Jesus.

What does a new view of Christ mean? Here's what I think:
• God was in Christ: "God...reconciled us to himself through Christ" (5:18). Before Christ came, God was not happy with people, and people were uncomfortable with God. Jesus changed that. "Reconcile" means to bring two estranged parties together. Christ's death, as I only dimly understand, put us at peace (reconciled) with God. If we get a right view of Jesus, we can get a right view of God.
• Christ died for all: "We are convinced that one has died for all" (5:15). Saul had been told that God despised Gentiles. A changed view of Jesus enlarged Paul's idea of "neighbor." The church is still struggling to help people realize that God values all people.
• A new view of Jesus changes us in fundamental ways: "He died for all, so that those who live might live no longer for themselves, but for him who died and was raised for them" (5:15). Jesus is pulling us out of our native selfishness toward a life of service.

II. A New Kind of Creation, 5:17.

"If anyone is in Christ, there is a new creation; everything old has passed away; see, everything has become new!" (5:17). Note the familiar phrase, "If anyone is IN CHRIST." Here are ways other commentators have written about "a new creation."
• Barclay seized on the "in Christ" idea to define what "a new creation" means: "Now to Paul the Christian is...in Christ, and therefore the old self of the Christian died in that death, and he

arose a new man, as new as if he had been freshly created by the hands of God" (*The Letters to the Corinthians*, 232).

• Kenneth Chafin quoted Peter Wagner, who said, "When I use the word Christian, I am referring to someone who is committed to the person of Christ, the body of Christ, and to the work of Christ" (*1, 2 Corinthians*, The Communicator's Commentary [Waco: Word Books, 1985], 240).

• James Reid put it this way: " 'A man in Christ' is Paul's definition of a Christian. Nothing less is adequate, for it implies an inner change, which is equivalent to a new creation. He is not merely improved, or reformed, or altered in any way which implies no more than an external change, however great; he is remade. He is different even from what he was at his best. The change is radical; it goes to the root of his being" (*The Interpreter's Bible*, vol. 10, 338).

After defining "a new creation," we need to apply it to our lives. If I am "in Christ" and "a new creation," I am different from what I was before. Here's how that plays out:

• My security is not in money or position. My security is in the caring providence of God.

• I'm not as interested in fun, pleasure, and entertainment as I was; I'm more on the serious side of life. Duty and service are not only my passion; they are my pleasure. My idea of what's good has changed and so has my idea of what is fun.

• I read my life through a different lens. Hard times are no longer just "tough luck." They are ways God is tempering me for service.

The problem with "a new creation" is in finding a Christian who has measured up to the definition. Here is where I tamper with Paul. I believe everything Paul said about Jesus. I have some reservation with what he said about us. When I became a Christian, God began saving me. By the inch, God is making me a "new creation." I am a work in process. This accounts for the times when I revert back to "the old man," when I am less than I profess to be. I'm not proud of those times, and I hope I am a better Christian today than I was twenty years ago. Am I "a new creation"? Sometimes. At other times, I'm not a very good illustration of what a Christian ought to be.

My disclaimer makes it sound like Christians are people who are "trying to be a new creation." In part, this is so, but it is not the whole story. I've seen children profess faith, grow up in the church, graduate, marry and start their families, and get started in business. The faith they professed as children has instructed them all their lives. They are different because they gave their hearts to Christ a long time ago. They are the people they are today because in some measure they are "in Christ." This is not just Paul's high-flown language; this is a higher way of life. I've seen it work.

III. A New Reason for Living, 5:18b-20.

"God...has given us the ministry of reconciliation; that is, in Christ God was reconciling the world to himself...and entrusting the message of reconciliation to us. So we are ambassadors for Christ, since God is making his appeal through us; we entreat you on behalf of Christ, be reconciled to God" (5:18b-20). In this brief quotation, Paul was doing two things:

(1) He was explaining himself. This text identifies Paul as an ambassador for Christ. His message was about how humankind could be put right with God; the very subject should command an audience.

(2) There is an assignment for everyone who is "a new creation." What Jesus fleshed out in his life, death, and resurrection and what Paul lived out in his missionary life of service are unfinished. Paul believed he was an extension of the work of Jesus. When I am at my best, I am an extension of what Paul was about.

As a boy I was taught, "We are ambassadors for Christ" (5:20a). When I was a senior in high school the combination of a godly home, good church experience, and Bible verses like this became a way for God to speak to me. The spirit of God impressed upon me that I should become a preacher. I was to "be an ambassador for Christ." I did not jump at "the call," but the idea would not go away, and finally I committed myself to prepare for the ministry. Ministers represent Christ.

Now take this idea to a higher plane. Is the calling to be an "ambassador for Christ" just for clergy? The early church gave laity liberty in telling about Jesus; all were under the authority of the apostles. Preachers don't do all the ministry. The laity does most of the work. When the laity is at its best, "they are ambassadors for Christ." There is enormous dignity in the idea that God would use you and me to extend God's kingdom. God has acted to save me. I can imitate God and act to save another. It is high service—and the only right response for all God in Christ has done for me.

Notes

Notes

www.ingramcontent.com/pod-product-compliance
Lightning Source LLC
Chambersburg PA
CBHW060719030426
42337CB00017B/2921